THE
Archive Photographs
SERIES

HAWKER
AIRCRAFT LTD

Young Tom Sopwith during his early days with aeroplanes. He holds a pipe which he stopped smoking (under duress) only when he was preparing to race or to make an important flight.

THE
Archive Photographs
SERIES

HAWKER
AIRCRAFT LTD

Compiled by
Derek N James IEng, AMRAeS

CHALFORD

First published 1996
Copyright © Derek N. James, 1996

The Chalford Publishing Company
St Mary's Mill, Chalford,
Stroud, Gloucestershire, GL6 8NX

ISBN 0 7524 0367 2

Typesetting and origination by
The Chalford Publishing Company
Printed in Great Britain by
Redwood Books, Trowbridge

*For all those who hold dear
their memories of
Hawker Aircraft Ltd*

By the same author:
Gloster Aircraft Company
Bristol Aeroplane Company

Other titles in the *Archive Photographs Aviation* series:
Avro
Boulton Paul Aircraft
Bristol Aeroplane Company
Filton and the Flying Machine
Gloster Aircraft Company
Shorts Aircraft

in preparation:
Blackburn Aircraft
De Havilland
Croydon Airport
Dornier
Dowty Aerospace
Hendon to Farnborough SBAC Displays 1932-1975
Handley Page
Junkers
Percivals Aircraft
SAAB
Supermarine
Vickers
Westland

Contents

Prologue   7

1.   Genesis and the Radials   9

2.   Mostly in-line Biplanes   23

3.   Windy Monoplanes   53

4.   The Jet Set   89

Acknowledgements   128

Harry Hawker, whose surname prefixed more Royal Air Force single-engined aircraft than any other manufacturer.

The best known of all Sopwith World War One aircraft is the Camel fighter. Sopwith Aviation and eight other companies produced 5,747 of them.

Prologue

Like all the best stories, the one about Hawker Aircraft Ltd begins, 'Once upon a time, many years ago...'. It is over a century now since Thomas Octave Murdoch Sopwith was born. As the schoolboy son of a wealthy civil engineer, young Tom loved motorcycles. Later he received engineering training and progressed to motorcars and motorboats. His two sisters were well-placed socially and he mixed with equally adventurous and wealthy young people. With them he had a brief flirtation – with ballooning – and all this before he was 21 years old!

The most important date of the early part of his life was 18 September 1910, the day when he 'discovered' powered flying. During the next two years he learned to fly, set up flying schools, bought and flew his own aeroplanes, and designed, built and tested others. In this latter venture he was joined by Fred Sigrist, a marine mechanic employed to tend Sopwith's motor yacht for £2 10s per week, and by Australian Harry Hawker, a young pilot who had gained his pilot's wings at a Sopwith flying school. With them, in 1912, he formed Sopwith Aviation Co. using a former skating-rink building in Kingston-upon-Thames.

When World War One began in August 1914 the company already had gained valuable experience in building aeroplanes. Throughout that war more than 12,000 Sopwith fighters and bombers were built by the company and by some thirty other manufacturers for the Allied Forces.

The euphoria following the outbreak of peace in November 1918 was fairly short-lived. The harsh economic climate of 'the Country fit for heroes to live in' brought almost a complete cessation of work for Britain's vast aircraft industry. On 3 September 1920 Sopwith Aviation closed its doors while still solvent, and went into voluntary liquidation – but paid its creditors every penny owed to them.

For the rest of the Hawker story (which could so easily have been the Sigrist Story) read on.

On His Majesty's Service. Members of Sopwith Aviation's Woodworkers Department – the 'chippies' – face the camera during a social event at a local hotel in August 1915.

One

Genesis and the Radials

It took more than voluntary liquidation and a shut-down to ground the Sopwith-Sigrist-Hawker triumvirate for long. Almost immediately a new organisation was being planned using part of the old premises – but not the old name. Harry Hawker's name was adopted instead. Thus H.G. Hawker Engineering Co. Ltd (HECo) was registered on 15 November 1920 with £20,000 capital. Its directors were F.I. Bennett, H.G. Hawker, Tom Sopwith, Fred Sigrist and V.W. Eyre. The company's business was building motorcycles, motorcars, engines – and aircraft! While motorbikes and cars got HECo going, its Board was keen to build aeroplanes again. The wish partly came true with contracts to recondition war-weary Sopwith Snipes and other aircraft.

Sadly, Harry Hawker was not to see the company grow. On 12 July 1921 his Nieuport Goshawk crashed while practising for the Aerial Derby. The victim of a tubercular spine, it was believed that he haemorrhaged in a tight racing turn and died before the Goshawk hit the ground.

Appointed chief designer in 1922, ginger-bearded ex-Royal Navy Capt B. 'Tommy' Thomson quickly (almost too quickly it proved) designed two radial-engined types: the Duiker, a two-seat reconnaissance aircraft with an unusual parasol wing, and the Woodcock, a single-seat biplane night fighter. Both were evaluated at the Aircraft Experimental Establishment (AEE) at Martlesham Heath; both were near disasters. The Duiker was almost uncontrollable and was abandoned; the tubby little Woodcock had poor handling characteristics and its wing fluttered in flight. But some bright spark at AEE saw that it had possibilities!

Capt Thompson was soon replaced by W. George Carter (who was later, as chief designer at Gloster Aircraft Co., to design the Meteor jet fighter). He re-jigged the Woodcock and turned it into a well-regarded fighter when operated by Nos 3 and 17 Squadrons. Since then the RAF has never been without a Hawker aeroplane on its inventory.

By this time HECo had occupied all of the Canbury Park Road site for Woodcock production plus Camel and Snipe reconstruction. Of more long-term importance was the arrival, in November 1923, of a young draughtsman named Sydney (later Sir Sydney) Camm, who was to stamp his design genius on the company for the next forty-three years. Born in Windsor, his early interest in aeroplanes was soon evinced when he began making flying models. In 1912, aged 19, he helped to form, and became secretary of, the Windsor Model Aeroplane Club and worked on the design and building of a man-carrying glider. During World War One he was employed by the Martinsyde Co., remaining with that company until he joined HECo. While George Carter was busy with the Hedgehog and Horsley, Camm was given responsibility for the little Cygnet civil two-seater project which weighed only 373lb. Two were built and they won prizes in several air races.

Meanwhile, the 1924 Hedgehog three-seater fleet reconnaissance aircraft with a 380 hp Bristol Jupiter radial engine had flown. During AEE evaluation its handling won unqualified approval. But changing requirements were its downfall.

Similarly, only one Hornbill single-seat fighter was built. Of wood and metal construction, it was powered by a 698 hp Rolls-Royce Condor in-line liquid-cooled engine. But when AEE pilots criticised its handling, said the cockpit was too small, and that it wouldn't climb above 24,000 ft, the Hornbill was not ordered.

Following studies of all-metal structures, in 1925 Sigrist and Camm produced a system of metal airframe construction which became the basis of all Hawker structures until 1943.

Designing military aircraft became Camm's prime task, starting with the Danecock, a revamped Woodcock for Denmark. Three were produced by HECo and made newspaper headlines when they left Croydon on their delivery flight to Denmark. Later, a dozen, renamed Dankok, were licence-built by Copenhagen's Royal Naval Dockyard in 1927-28. Camm also got the job of refining the Woodcock. Using all-metal construction and named Heron, it earned much praise during AEE evaluation but failed to win orders. Later the prototype was entered for the Kings Cup Race, but as it taxied to the start line it collided with a parked motorcar! Exit the Heron.

Hawker moved up a size with the next design, the Horsley, named after Tom Sopwith's Horsley Towers home. This last Carter-designed HECo aeroplane was a big two-seat day bomber/torpedo carrier. Powered by a 660 hp Rolls-Royce Condor in-line engine, the first versions of 1926 were the last of HECo's wooden aeroplanes. Later Horsleys were either wood/metal or all-metal. In total 124 of them were built for the RAF, the Greek Naval Air Service and, named Dantorp, for Denmark.

The next two types to be built, the Hawfinch single-seat fighter and the Harrier two-seater bomber/torpedo carrier, were built only as prototypes, but both added to HECo's storehouse of aerodynamic and structures know-how. Then, in June 1928, the first Hart bomber flew. It was something else!

Harry Hawker in a 150 hp Sunbeam racing car near one of the steeply banked turns of the famed Brooklands race track.

The offices of Sopwith Aviation Co. in Canbury Park Road, Kingston-upon-Thames, were used by Hawker Engineering Co. and Hawker Aircraft Ltd from 1920 to 1959. A small part of this building has been retained as a reminder of the company's links with the town.

Overhaul and conversion of Sopwith Snipes at the Canbury Park Road works in about 1921.

Fred Sigrist was originally employed to look after Tom Sopwith's motor yacht. Inevitably, however, he became involved with aeroplanes and ultimately achieved great things as a highly skilled aeronautical engineer.

The Duiker reconnaissance parasol monoplane proved almost uncontrollable in the air. After only eighteen hours flying it was abandoned – and not a moment too soon!

This view of the Duiker shows its swept-back wings. The supporting struts would sometimes break loose from each other due to massive aileron flutter.

Sydney Camm, who joined Hawker Engineering Co. in November 1923 and was appointed chief engineer thirty-six years later, at Byfleet in 1915. At that time he was employed by the Martinsyde Co. and was secretary of the Windsor Model Aeroplane Club. He holds a canard configuration monoplane with twin elastically-powered pusher propellers.

The first Woodcock II, with single-bay wings and machine guns beside the cockpit. Individual 'helmets' on the engine cylinders were first thoughts on ways to prevent valve gear icing.

A Woodcock II night fighter at Brooklands in July 1925. Heat from the exhaust collector ring on the 380 hp Bristol Jupiter engine helped prevent the valve gear icing up on chilly nights.

No. 17 Sqdn's motto was 'By day and by night'. Here its Woodcock II night fighters fly by day from RAF Upavon in June 1927. Note the flight leader's pennant on his aircraft's tail, and the black zigzag squadron markings.

The diminutive two-seat Cygnet, G-EBMB, with a 34 hp British Anzani engine. One of two built, it is seen here with Sydney Camm (left), H.J. Jones and P.W.S. 'George' Bulman resplendent in plus-fours at Lympne in 1926.

The same Cygnet G-EBMB, pictured here at Dunsfold in the early 1950s, weighed only 373 lb. It is now in the RAF Museum at Hendon with other Hawker aeroplanes designed by Sydney Camm.

Frank Murphy, Hawker test pilot, flies the Cygnet over Langley. The headgear appears to be either a beret or a back-to-front cap.

Prickly customer. The 1924 three-seat Hedgehog maritime reconnaissance aircraft got glowing flight test reports. But the Air Ministry wouldn't buy it because it didn't perform any better than existing types.

Everything had hinges on the Jupiter-engined Hedgehog. On the ground its wings folded; in flight the ailerons drooped and there were flaps on top and bottom wings.

Designed by W. George Carter, the Hornbill fighter was the first Hawker aeroplane with an in-line liquid-cooled engine, the 698 hp Rolls-Royce Condor. It had a 190 m.p.h. top speed.

The Hornbill's slow speed handling, advanced metal and wood construction and sleek lines were outweighed by basic faults like the too-small cockpit and poor high speed manoeuvrability. It wasn't ordered.

This Dankok, No. 158, built by the Danish Royal Navy Dockyard in 1927, survived World War Two and was restored for display in Copenhagen Museum.

Third, and last, Hawker-built Danecock, powered by a 385 hp Armstrong Siddeley Jaguar engine at Brooklands in 1926. A dozen more were licence-built in Denmark with the name Dankok.

The tin fighter. Hawker's first all-metal aircraft, the Heron fighter, won high praise from RAF test pilots but didn't enter production.

First it was named the Kingston, then the Horsley after Tom Sopwith's Horsley Towers home. This two-seat torpedo/bomber equipped six RAF squadrons. These await delivery to No. 100 Sqdn at RAF Spittlegate.

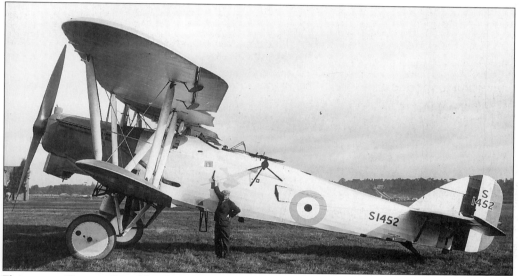

Flying tug. Seen at Brooklands in 1931, this Horsley II, with a 665 hp Rolls-Royce Condor engine, was a target tug. The wind-driven winch is on the fuselage side.

An Armstrong Siddeley Leopard engine powers this Horsley, one of several used as engine flying test-beds between 1926 and 1938. It was virtually the prototype of the Dantorp for Denmark.

The Dantorp naval three-seater torpedo/bomber was a modified Horsley. Two pattern aircraft, of which this is the first, were delivered to the Danish Government in 1933.

The second Dantorp, carrying a torpedo, shows its versatility. Here, with its crew of three, it flies with a wheeled undercarriage...

... and here, mounted on floats, it is lowered into chilly Danish waters by the good ship *Ingolf's* crane. Though extensively test flown, these pattern aircraft failed to spark off licensed production in Denmark.

A 450 hp Jupiter engine, metal propeller and a 171 m.p.h. top speed all failed to win orders for the 1927 Hawfinch fighter. But they helped shape Sydney Camm's future fighter designs.

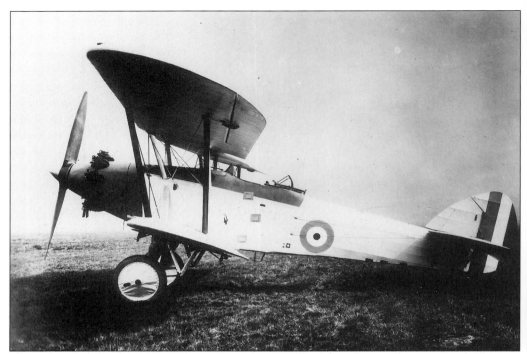

The first Hawker aeroplane named Harrier was a 1926 day torpedo/bomber which failed because its 583 hp Jupiter engine simply wasn't man enough to get this fully-laden three ton aeroplane into the air!

The sole, but really useful, Harrier. Though it failed to win orders it went on to do good work as a flying test bed for the Bristol Orion and Hydra radial engines.

Two
Mostly in-line Biplanes

The Hart heralded a new era of aircraft development for Hawker and a new concept of flying for the RAF. Intended as a replacement for ageing DH9As and Fairey Fawns in RAF squadrons, the prototype, with a top speed of 184 m.p.h. and a Rolls-Royce F.XIB in-line engine, was higher than the specified requirement. Some 960 were built during 1929-36, initially equipping No. 13 Sqdn in January 1930. Hart bomber and trainer versions then served for a decade with fourteen RAF and fifteen RAFVR squadrons and units, three University Air Squadrons, and many other units. Harts were exported to four countries and licence-built in Sweden. Subsequent HECo aeroplanes based on the Hart include many renowned types – as if the Hart had borne multiple young fawns!

But before that happy event there was the little 1928 Tomtit ab initio trainer, of which twenty-four were built for the RAF. It had design goodies such as Handley-Page slots and a Reid and Sigrist blind flying panel. A handful were built for sport flying. Two went to Canada and one to New Zealand.

Then followed another trio of one-offs. First was the Hawker F.20/27 fighter with a Bristol Jupiter radial engine. Then came the Hoopoe naval fighter, tested with a variety of radial engines. Tail-end Charlie of the group was the handsome Hornet single-seater fighter, which showed what could be achieved, aesthetically and performance-wise (its top speed was 205 m.p.h.) with the use of a Rolls-Royce in-line engine. None were ordered, but the Hornet was the basis for the magnificent Fury.

In May 1931 No. 43 Sqdn at RAF Tangmere was the first of six squadrons to receive Furies, the first RAF fighters to exceed 200 m.p.h. HECo built 279 Furies, selling some to five overseas countries. Spanish and Yugoslav Furies had cantilever undercarriage legs and Dowty internally-sprung wheels – very pretty aeroplanes.

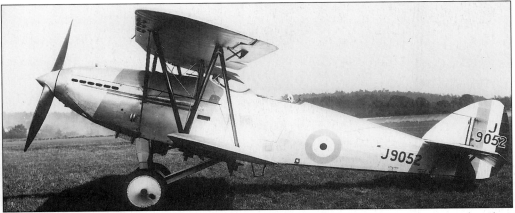

The magnificent 1928 Hart bomber prototype. With a 525 hp Rolls-Royce Kestrel in-line engine, it was a success from the outset. It served with twenty-one RAF and AAF squadrons and spawned some ten variants.

Then followed the many Hart and Fury lookalikes, all first flown by balding George Bulman, HECo's chief test pilot: the Nimrod single-seat naval fighter, which first joined 408 Flight in HMS Glorious in November 1931 and served with four more Flights and eight Fleet Air Arm (FAA) Squadrons; the 301 Demon two-seater fighters, which flew with sixteen UK-based and overseas RAF squadrons and were sold to Australia; the Osprey, the FAA's first fast two-seat reconnaissance aircraft, which joined Nimrods in several two-type squadrons from 1932, some serving until 1940. Sweden, Portugal and Spain bought seven Ospreys between them. In 1932 No. 4 Sqdn was the first of thirteen squadrons to get the Audax, an Army Cooperation version to support the 'Brown Jobs'. HECo built 265 and the Gloster, Bristol, Avro and Westland companies another 453. Some served until 1941 as glider tugs. All forty-seven Gloster-built Hardy general purpose aircraft spent their operational lives in the Middle East, one surviving until June 1941.

A brace of 1934 HECo-funded prototypes which failed to win orders were the PV.3, a near relation of the Fury, with spats and an evaporatively cooled Rolls-Royce Goshawk engine, and the PV.4 do-it-all general purpose type, with a Bristol Perseus radial engine. The following year HECo built four Hartbees two-seat ground-support aircraft as 'this-is-how-to-do-it' examples for the South African factory which licence-built sixty-five more. In 1934, too, came the much-loved Hind two-seat light bomber which embodied the best features of earlier Hawker biplanes. It equipped thirty-three RAF and Auxiliary Air Force (AAF) squadrons during 1935 to 1939 and was widely used as a trainer. Of 581 built over 200 new and ex-RAF aircraft went to some twelve overseas countries. Last of these many Hart derivatives was the Hector two-seat Army Cooperation aeroplane. As Rolls-Royce Kestrels had been earmarked for Hinds, a 805 hp Napier Dagger H-configuration air-cooled engine was used. Westland Aircraft built all 178 Hectors for the RAF.

To meet a requirement by the 'anchor clankers', in 1929 the Hart was temporarily modified with the folding wings like many naval aircraft. Note the banked Brooklands race track in the distance.

Canbury Park Road's sawmill in 1931. Cockpit decking, bulkheads and sections of wing can be seen.

Members of Hawker Engineering's Rib Shop, Plane Floor and Sawmill attend their Gentlemen's Evening in a Kingston hotel during 1932.

In 1934 the first production Hart, a Hawker trials aircraft, was fitted with the Frazer-Nash power-operated 'lobster-back' gun turret used in late production Demon two-seat fighters.

Hawker's own civil-registered Hart, which survived some forty years test flying, wartime ferrying, racing and display flying. It was also used for air-to-air photography, the camera man snug in the rear cockpit.

Hart type wings being assembled on the Plane Floor at Canbury Park Road. Note the wooden two-spar and multiple rib construction.

Now in the RAF Museum, Hart G-ABMR is seen in RAF markings being flown by Hawker pilot Duncan Simpson.

A snow job. This Hart, built by Vickers Aviation in 1933 and powered by a Bristol Pegasus engine, went to Canada for ski-landing gear trials in the following year.

Pilots and those who built the aircraft. Left to right: F. Middleton (chargehand), Philip Lucas, B. Haywood (foreman), A. Fordham (manager), 'George' Bulman, Gerry Sayer. This photograph may have been taken just before the 1932 Hendon RAF Pageant, when Lucas and Sayer flew in the rear cockpit of the company Hart, G-ABMR, fitted with spatted wheels.

Used by HAL and Bristol Aeroplane Co. for engine development flying, this Hart has a Pegasus engine in a long-chord cowling.

Harts of Nos 11 and 39 Sqdns RAF, based at Risalpur, India, fly over the Himalayas during 1933.

A Rolls-Royce test bed. This Hart's PV.12 in-line engine became the world-beating Merlin. Apart from the four-blade propeller, this installation resembles that of the later Merlin-powered Hurricane.

This first production dual-control Hart trainer went to No. 1 Flying Training School, RAF Leuchars, in mid-1933. It was written off when it dived into the ground in April 1941.

The nearest Hart (India), K3922, with red band markings, joined No. 11 Sqdn at Risalpur in May 1934. It overturned on landing at No. 1 Armament Training Unit at Bairagarh on 14 July 1942.

A Bristol Pegasus radial engine powers this Hart, the first of four delivered to Sweden in early 1934. Licensed production of Harts in Sweden began in 1935 and totalled forty-two aircraft.

One of eight Harts which were supplied to Estonia in 1933 complete with either wheeled or float landing gear.

Three of a group of fourteen Hart Specials in store in one of RAF Cardington's vast airship hangars during 1936. Also in the picture are two Vickers Vildebeests, a Saro Cloud, three folded Vickers Virginia Xs and several Avro Tutor wings.

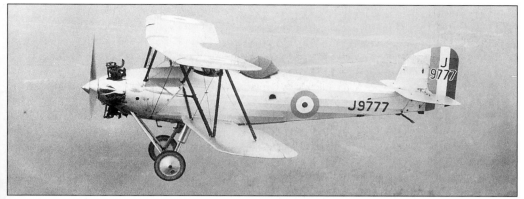

Two dozen Tomtit trainers with Armstrong Siddeley Mongoose radial engines were built for the RAF. Here a pupil pilot practises instrument flying under the hood in the rear cockpit. This aircraft, from No. 3 Flying Training School, was wrecked in a take-off accident on 14 July 1931.

Six Tomtits were built for civil flying. This one has a 115 hp Cirrus Hermes in-line air-cooled engine.

This Tomtit had a 150 hp Armstrong Siddeley Wolseley radial engine. It was flown by Hawker's Gerry Sayer in the 1933 King's Cup Race – but got nowhere!

The last Mongoose-powered Tomtit was originally K1786 in RAF service. Bought by Hawker after the war, it is seen here being flown by Neville Duke, who raced and demonstrated it on many occasions.

The 1927 F.20/27 had a Jupiter engine – which was its undoing. Its performance was inferior to other in-line engined prototypes and it was abandoned after turning over on landing at Farnborough in December 1931.

The Boo-Hoopoe. It was a 'crying' shame that the 1927 Hoopoe naval fighter was another HECo prototype which failed to make the big time. Note the original two-bay wings and Mercury radial engine.

Camm switched the Hoopoe to single-bay wings and an Armstrong Siddeley Jaguar engine – but in vain. The Hoopoe's younger and faster brother, the Nimrod, killed it off.

The sole Hornet, with its Rolls-Royce F.XIS in-line engine, was an outstanding example of streamlined efficiency, as this head-on view so clearly reveals – despite Brooklands' morning mists.

The Hornet lived its short thirteen-month life in the fast lane – until its top wing came off in a mid-air collision! But its design spawned the fabulous Fury fighters.

The first of twenty-one Furies built and delivered in three weeks in April 1931 to delight the RAF's fighter boys. This one, initially an evaluation aircraft, went to No. 1 Sqdn.

This Fury I flew with Nos 1, 25 and 43 Sqdns based at Tangmere and Hawkinge before becoming a ground instruction aircraft in November 1937.

Sqdn Ldr R.H. Hanmer, in Fury I, K1930, leads the nine aircraft of No. 43 Sqdn. Based at Tangmere, the squadron flew Furies from 1932 to 1938.

Fury fighters in production at Canbury Park Road works.

One of two Furies built at HECo's expense during 1931-32 was this Intermediate Fury, G-ABSE, used for trials of various engines and airframe systems and equipment.

Photographed at Brooklands in 1932, this Fury, with a 530 hp Armstrong Siddeley Panther radial engine, was bought by Norway for evaluation. It was temporarily flown with a ski undercarriage.

Bulman, in the Norwegian Fury, keeps a wary eye on the Hart photographic aircraft.

A dramatic photograph of the Norwegian Fury in its natural element.

Pilots four. Hawker pilots pictured astride the nose of the company's Hart during the mid-1930s. Left to right: 'Gerry' Sayer, who later joined Gloster Aircraft Co. as chief test pilot, Maurice Summers, Philip G. Lucas and P.W.S. 'George' Bulman.

In June 1934 three Furies were delivered to the Portuguese Army Air Force. This was the first to fly – on 28 May.

Three Hispano Suiza-engined Spanish Furies had cantilever undercarriage legs, made possible by Dowty internally-sprung wheels. Delivered in July 1936, they flew in the Civil War – occasionally for both sides!

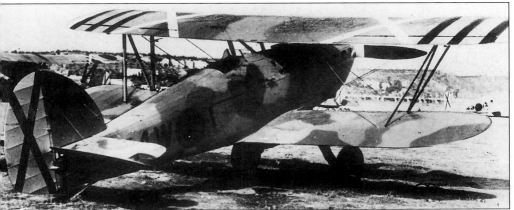

The first of the Spanish Furies, with a Hispano Suiza 12XBrs engine, seen here in Spain with Government Forces markings.

The handsome High Speed Fury was used to develop both the basic airframe design and Rolls-Royce's Kestrel and Goshawk engines. Note the spatted wheels and narrow parallel-chord top wings.

Originally named the Norn, a contraction of Naval Hornet, this 1930 naval carrier fighter prototype was renamed Nimrod. It led to production of eighty-seven Nimrods for thirteen FAA Squadron and Flights.

'Nimrod, Mighty Hunter Before The Lord'. The prototype photographed at Brooklands before its first test flight by HECo pilot 'Gerry' Sayer on 14 October 1931.

A 'two-piper' destroyer acting as 'plane-guard' hoists a Nimrod from the 'oggin' after it had crashed close to the carrier. The pilot was rescued by the destroyer's whaler crew.

The first of a pair of spatted Nimrods delivered to Denmark in 1934. They were intended as pattern aircraft to launch licensed production, but none were built there.

First production Demon two-seat fighter on Brooklands' grass airfield in February 1933. Interesting features are the long exhaust pipe, the cut-down gunner's cockpit, and his Lewis gun and mounting ring.

This Demon I flew with Nos 23 Sqdn at Biggin Hill and 604 Sqdn at Hendon between 1933 and 1939. Here its Kestrel IIS is being run-up by a Rolls-Royce engineer at Brooklands.

This folded two-seat naval reconnaissance Osprey flew with 803 Sqdn FAA in the carriers HMS *Eagle* and *Hermes* during 1932. Note the catapult spools at the fuselage bottom line.

A warship at sea catapult launches an Osprey I floatplane.

In 1936 these Ospreys equipped 711 Mediterranean Fleet Catapult Sqdn. Second from left is an Osprey III, the others are MkIICs. Sailors will instantly note the differing water rudder profiles!

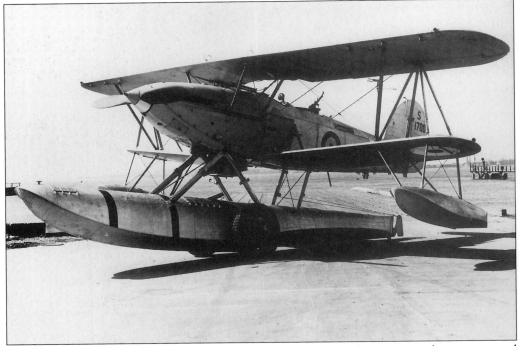

Stainless steel was used in the construction of Osprey IIIs, to combat corrosion by seawater and the salty environment. This one has a single main float with underwing stabiliser floats.

This 1932 Audax I Army Cooperation aircraft served with the RAF's School where pilots learned that sort of flying. His shiny pate instantly identifies 'George' Bulman, HECo's chief test pilot, who eschewed flying helmets.

In 1934 Persia placed a repeat order for twenty-six Audaxes with Bristol Pegasus engines. This is one of them.

One Armstrong Siddeley Panther engine-powered Audax went to the Egyptian Air Force – but no one seems to know if another bunch was delivered as well!

Hardy annual. Designed by Camm, built as a Hart, and converted to the Hardy general purpose aircraft by Vickers. Note the wing-mounted camera (or is it a smoke-generator?) and underwing supplies containers. All forty-seven Hardies were built by Gloster Aircraft.

Private Venture becomes Major Disappointment. The 1934 PV.3 had a hefty 700 hp Rolls-Royce Goshawk engine, four guns, spats and a 224 m.p.h. top speed – but these weren't enough to win it orders.

The last of four 1935 Hartbees ground support aircraft destined for South Africa; sixty-five more were licence-built in Pretoria. The South African Air Force flew them until 1946.

The Hind light bomber bridged the gap between the Hart and delivery of Britain's modern monoplane bombers which were still several years down the road.

Engine al fresco. The third and last Yugoslav Hind with uncowled 800 hp French Gnome-Rhone Mistral radial engine. The earlier pair had 690 hp Rolls-Royce Kestrel XVI engines.

Not as 'Nazi' as it appears: the last of three Latvian Hinds with Bristol Mercury engines. Latvia's swastika, a good luck emblem, was blue; the 'nasty one' was black.

A bomb-carrying Hind, one of four ordered by Portugal, photographed at Brooklands in 1936.

One of 178 Hector Army cooperation aircraft built by Westland Aircraft in 1936-37. Note the Napier Dagger engine, message pick-up hook on the undercarriage, and the underwing stores containers.

Unlucky for some! This Hector joined No. 13 Sqdn at RAF Odiham in February 1937 but ran out of fuel and crashed near Farnborough four months later.

Three
The Stormy Monoplanes

The years spanned by those Hawker biplanes are regarded by many as a golden era, when the RAF was 'the best flying club in the world'. But the sleeker, faster, more effective monoplanes were knocking at the door of every design office. Camm's first crack at this configuration in Autumn 1933 was a low-wing design, the Fury Monoplane, with a fixed trousered undercarriage and four guns. Early in 1934 the Rolls-Royce PV.12 in-line liquid-cooled engine (later to become the renowned Merlin) replaced the evaporatively-cooled Goshawk, a retractable undercarriage was embodied plus an enclosed cockpit. The fuselage structure was the proven Camm/Sigrist steel tube frame, with wooden formers providing curved external shape; its wings and tail unit were all-metal structures and the aircraft was fabric-covered. HECo submitted this modified design, known as the F36/34 fighter, to the Air Ministry in September and five months later won a contract to build one. This aeroplane, the forerunner of the Hurricane, powered by a 1,029 hp Merlin and with provision for eight wing-mounted guns, was first flown on 6 November 1935 by George Bulman.

Meanwhile, in 1933, the company's name was changed to Hawker Aircraft Ltd (HAL). The following year it bought Gloster Aircraft Co. (GAC) which had one of the largest UK aircraft factories near Gloucester, and in 1935, with great expansion of the RAF forecast, formed a Trust to buy Armstrong Siddeley Development Co. and established Hawker Siddeley Aircraft Ltd. This powerful consortium included HAL, Gloster, Sir W.G. Armstrong Whitworth Aircraft, Armstrong Siddeley Motors, A.V. Roe and Co. and Air Service Training. New aircraft were soon being built in these factories, which began to bulge at the seams. So Hawker borrowed £30,000 and built another at Langley, Bucks. While still producing biplanes against earlier orders, the consortium's growing financial muscle enabled it to develop the F36/34 into the Hurricane, which was to become the most deadly and successful piece of Great Britain's defences in the Battle of Britain, its pilots destroying more enemy aircraft than all the other fighters and ground defences put together.

In June 1936 HAL received an order for 600 Hurricanes. The first flew in October 1937 and deliveries to No. 111 Sqdn at Northolt began two months later. Early Hurricanes had 1,030 hp Merlin engines and fabric-covered wings, but metal was used from about the 430th. This work quickly filled the Kingston, Brooklands and Langley factories, and when an order for 1,000 was received in November 1938, sub-contract work went to GAC, which built 2,450 Hurricanes.

When World War Two came on 3 September 1939, some 500 Hurricanes had reached the RAF. By 8 August 1940, when the first shots were fired in the Battle of Britain, production rate was eight aircraft per day and 1,350 Hurricanes had been delivered to equip thirty-two of Fighter Command's fifty-two interceptor squadrons. Throughout the war Hurricanes fought in every operational theatre, operating from grass and snow airfields, concrete runways, desert and jungle strips, being catapulted from merchant ships to protect convoys and, as Sea Hurricanes, flying from aircraft carriers. The Hurricane's armament was increased to twelve guns, and some had four 20 mm or two 40 mm cannon for 'tank busting'. Others carried two 500 lb bombs, eight rocket projectiles (RPs) or external fuel tanks. More powerful engines were installed, later Hurricanes having the 1,650 hp Merlin 27 driving a four-blade Rotol propeller. There was even a biplane Hurricane! It had a jettisonable top wing to provide extra lift at take-off but the experiment, not altogether surprisingly, was abandoned. By the end of the war some 15,000

It destroyed more hostiles in the Battle of Britain than all other defences put together. It was the RAF's first 300 m.p.h. fighter. This was the first of 15,000 built. They named it Hurricane.

Hurricanes had been built in the UK and Canada. They were supplied to fourteen other countries. Some 3,000 aircraft were despatched by sea to the Red Air Force, though numbers were lost in convoys en route.

Designed at the same time as the Hurricane and sharing its outer wings and tailplane, the Henley light bomber came a poor second to its stablemate in the Air Ministry's eyes. It never dropped a bomb in anger, being relegated to target-towing duties before its three-year RAF service began in late 1939. Gloster built all 200. Another HAL aeroplane which soon bit the dust was the Hotspur two-seat turret fighter, basically a Henley clasping a Boulton Paul gun turret to its back. It was the last Hawker prototype to be built and flown at Brooklands, which site the company quit in 1940, production now being based at Canbury Park Road and Langley.

Next in HAL's fighter family came a pair of almost identical twins: the 400 m.p.h. Typhoon and Tornado powered by a 2,100 hp Napier Sabre and a 1,760 hp Rolls-Royce Vulture respectively. The first to fly, on 6 December 1939, was the Tornado – an all-metal construction with a monocoque type rear fuselage having no internal bracing. The pilot was HAL's Philip Lucas. This early start, however, was to no avail. The Vulture engine was a minor disaster and, finally, the Tornado was abandoned. The Typhoon, which Lucas flew on 24 February 1940, suffered its own engine troubles and structural failure problems. These continued after production of this burly six-ton fighter had been begun at GAC, where, on 27 May 1941, that company's test pilot, Michael Daunt, flew the first of 3,312 Typhoons built there. Entering RAF service in September 1941 with No. 56 Sqdn at Duxford, it initially proved unpopular with pilots, its performance as an interceptor being disappointing. However, things got better. In service with thirty RAF squadrons, it earned a fearsome reputation as a close support aircraft, its four 20 mm cannon, RPs or 1,000 lb bombs demolishing ground targets such as trains, bridges, gun emplacements and road vehicles. In the Caen and Falaise battle it devastated enemy tank formations with rocket projectiles, clearing the way for Allied armies to advance. The Tempest, with a thinner, almost elliptical wing, longer fuselage and a new tail, was aesthetically more pleasing, its top speed went up to 446 m.p.h. and its handling characteristics were better. Apart from the fifty built by Bristol Aeroplane Co, the 1,394 Tempests were built at HAL's Langley factory. They were produced in two forms: 942 with Napier Sabre engines for UK-based squadrons, and the remainder with Bristol Centaurus radials which operated mainly overseas. Like the Typhoon they were used as ground attack aircraft, but earned their spurs tackling the V1 flying bombs aimed at the British Isles in 1944. Tempests destroyed more than thirty per cent of the RAF's tally of 1,771 between June and September.

A pair of HAL fighters evolved from the Tornado/Typhoon/Tempest clan was the Fury, an RAF Tempest replacement. Although peace put a stop on RAF orders, development of the Sea Fury for the FAA continued. The first flew on 21 February 1945; it had an arrester hook, but the folding wings and other 'anchor-clanker' requirements came later. Some 720 Sea Fury fighters and trainers were built and the type saw action in Korea, its naval pilots fighting with great distinction. Sea Furies were sold to six overseas countries and licence-built in Holland.

The prototype Hurricane first flew on 6 November 1935. The hinged wheel doors and tailplane struts were soon discarded, the retractable tailwheel was fixed down and metal replaced fabric on the wings. And that was just for starters!

Brooklands 1938. Hurricane production goes on in the foreground and right; on the far left are the upper centre section of Hinds being built for Afghanistan and Persia. Facing the camera on the right is works manager Harry Patrick. Compare the Hurricane structure with that of the Furies on page 38.

During early 1939 twelve Hurricane Is were supplied to Yugoslavia. This one is showing off its fabric-covered wings, neatly-stowed undercarriage – and lots of oil leaks from the engine bay.

Hurricane I, L1557, was exhibited in the Brussels Salon Aeronautique in July 1939. It crashed near Biggin Hill on 9 August while serving with No. 111 Sqdn. Alongside is the special 'Speed Spitfire'.

Originally L1606, this early Hurricane I was returned to Hawkers, then civil registered and first flown with these markings in September 1939. It was used to test fly new equipment and design features.

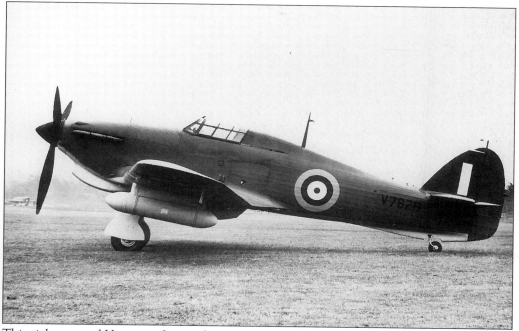

This eight-gunned Hurricane I carried extra fuel tanks for long-distance flying and a carburetter air filter under the nose. Sand in the sump was bad news for Rolls-Royce's Merlin engines.

'Mmm – that's cosy.' Keeping a Hurricane's engine and propeller hub warm was easy with this heater and giant muff – once you'd discovered where all the press-studs fitted.

A Sea Hurricane, with everything dangling, over a carrier's deck. The pilot is either getting a check that flaps, undercarriage and hook are down or has had a wave-off to have another go at landing-on.

No. 274 Sqdn's Hurricane Is at Amrita, Egypt, in November 1940. The nearest one in the line-up, P2544, is a Gloster-built aircraft...

... as is this singleton, P2627, of the same squadron, seen over the desert while based at Sidi Hanesh in November 1940.

This Hurricane I had a three-blade metal propeller. British built 'Hurris' had two-blade wooden Watts propellers or three-blade de Havilland or Rotol propellers. Note the gun ports in the wing.

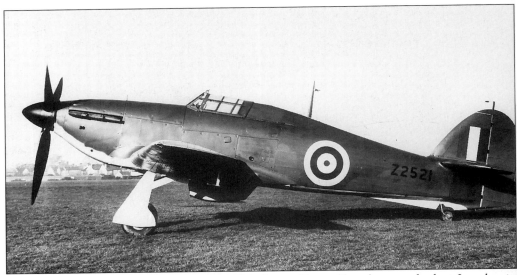

A longer nose enhanced this Hurricane IIA Series 2's profile, photographed at Langley in December 1940. Its 342 m.p.h. top speed made it the fastest Hurricane variant. Note the bead sight on the engine cowling.

The Hillson Slip-wing Hurricane I, L1884. An experimental second wing was fitted in 1942 for additional take-off lift. It was then jettisoned. This 'biplane' Hurricane was flown a few times, but the project was abandoned.

'We hunt by day and night.' – No. 85 Sqdn's motto. And it did, flying Hurricane Is by day in the Battle of Britain then night ops from Church Fenton, Yorks, afterwards.

This Gloster-built Hurricane IIB was one of 2,952 Hurricanes sent to the Red Air Force during World War Two. Its tropical carburetter air filter seems unnecessary for Soviet snows!

In 1940-41 Gloster Aircraft, under sub-contract from Hawker, built a Hurricane every five hours round the clock. The wooden formers which clad the fuselage's tubular structure are awaiting fabric covering.

'Our John'. This cannon-armed Hurricane IIB, BN795, was given to the RAF by his mother in memory of Squadron Leader John Gillan. He once flew a wind-assisted Hurricane from Edinburgh to Northolt averaging 408 m.p.h.!

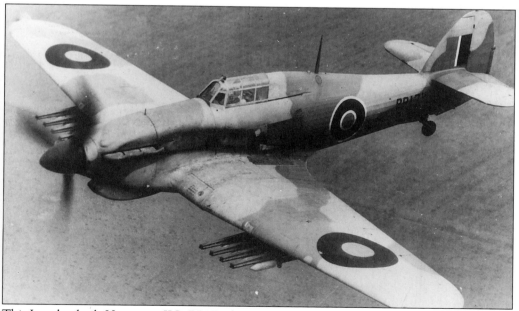

This Langley-built Hurricane IIC, BP173, has a tropical carburetter air intake and carries eight underwing 60 lb rocket projectiles.

Hurri in a bonnet – or protective cockpit cover. Note the venturi tube, which provided slipstream power to some instruments on the blind flying panel.

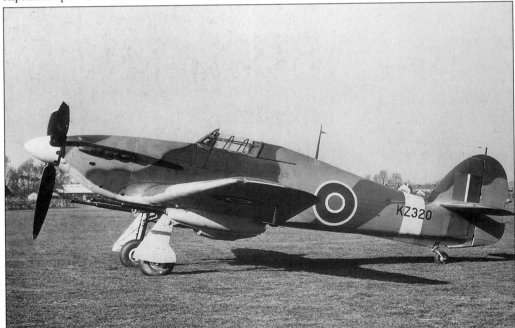

Flying tin-opener. Armed with two 40 mm Rolls-Royce BF or, like this one, Vickers S cannon, 'tank-busting' Hurricane IIDs were used with great success in North Africa and Burma.

Empty cases cascade from this Hurricane's eight guns which, with engine running, are fired in the butts at a desert airfield in 1941.

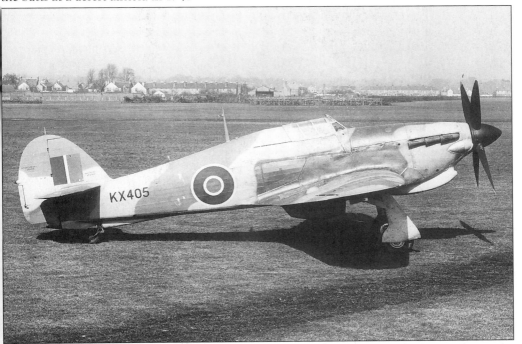

This Hurricane V's 1635 hp Merlin 27 turned a four-blade Rotol propeller. Note the intake below the exhausts for cooling air to engine accessories.

Off with the spinner and on with the skis. This 1942 Canadian-built Hurricane XII had a Packard-built Merlin engine, US-built Hamilton propeller and twelve wing-mounted guns.

The classic Hawker fuselage structure revealed in this photograph of 'nude' Hurricane LF751 during restoration in 1988 by the Royal Aeronautical Society's Medway Branch.

An era ends at Langley. This photograph of the last few Hurricanes being built was taken in March 1944. 'The Last of the Many', PZ865, a Hurricane IIC, is nearest the camera. The classic Hawker fuselage structure is clearly seen.

'From the First of the Few to the Last of the Thousands' proclaim the banners – which also carry the Hurricane's 'battle honours' – on PZ865, nearing completion at Langley.

'The Last of the Many', with a few of the many who built them. Left to right: Bill Miles, Fred Bromley, Arthur Arculus, -?-, Jasper Lewis, Charles Clarke, -?-, Fred Glindon.

The last Hurricane was ceremoniously 'rolled out' from the Langley factory in 1944. It is seen here with many of the Hawker employees who had helped to build some 15,000 Hurricanes during World War Two.

Hurricane PZ865 was an eye-catching part of Kingston-on-Thames Victory Parade on Saturday 8 June 1946. The route was Portsmouth Road, Eden and Brook Streets, Orchard Road, Fairfield South, and Hawkes and Cambridge Roads before dispersing in Douglas Road.

After World War Two a number of ex-RAF Hurricane IICs were sold to Persia as fighter trainers. This was one of them.

The final example of the Hurricane in its natural element. Note the whip aerial replacing the standard rigid type.

'Who's got a shiny nose, then?' The ill-fated Henley light bomber prototype airborne from Brooklands in 1937.

When the Air Ministry moved the goalposts, Henleys towed targets across the skies. Result? Overheated engines and crashes. This second prototype already has a wind-driven towing winch.

Based on the Henley, the 1938 Hotspur turret-fighter was pipped at the post (some would say 'beaten by several lengths') by the Boulton Paul Defiant, and only one Hotspur was built.

Sydney Camm (seated) and R.H. 'Roy' Chaplin, assistant chief designer, study a general arrangement drawing of the Hotspur's fuselage. Chaplin was an important but often forgotten figure in the Hawker design hierarchy.

The Hotspur's gun-turret was only a mock-up and was later removed. This aeroplane then earned its corn helping with Henley development.

The Rolls-Royce Vulture-engined Tornado I prototype with a Rotol Airscrews six-blade contra-rotating propeller at Staverton in September 1942. Jock McLean, a Rotol engineer, strides in front of the aeroplane.

HG641, the 'bitza' Tornado fourth prototype (built from 'bitza' Typhoon rear fuselage and wings), was powered by a 2,200 hp Bristol Centaurus air-cooled radial engine. It was used for Typhoon development flying.

The Typhoon, a burly five-ton 1940 fighter with a bulky 2,000 hp Napier Sabre engine. Note this first prototype's small fin and metal-faired canopy.

The second prototype Typhoon, with 12-gun wings, window in canopy fairing and hinged wheel-bay doors (later abandoned) on the undercarriage leg fairings.

The second Typhoon, now with four 20 mm Hispano cannon and a larger fin. The 400 m.p.h. 'Tiffie' was on its way to being an ace ground support aircraft – the soldiers' friend.

Going left to right, Typhoon IB EK497 reveals rocket projectiles and cannon, ideal for unzipping tanks and locos...

... and going right to left shows car-type cockpit doors and large radiator. Black/white under-wing recognition stripes did not prevent this No. 183 Sqdn aircraft being shot down by a US Air Force Mustang fighter over Belgium on New Year's Day 1945!

During most of 1943 No. 183 Sqdn's Tiffie-bombers carried two 1,000 lb bombs on underwing racks, empty here on HF-L. Note the sliding clear-view canopy and enclosed cannon.

Though originally named Typhoon II, following a new engine installation and wing shape this became the Tempest I. Surprisingly, this 1943 prototype retained the early Typhoon's cockpit doors and canopy.

HAL pilot Bill Humble shows off the clean lines of the Sabre-engined Tempest I prototype. The leading edge wing radiators and later clear view canopy are noteworthy.

Close-up of a Tempest V showing wide-track Dowty undercarriage, 'chin' radiator, central carburetter air intake, four-blade Rotol propeller and four 'in-wing' cannons.

Like peas in a pod. Apart from the 'chin' radiator and cockpit canopy, the Tempest I and this Tempest V prototype were markedly similar.

The Office. Pilot's eye-view of a Tempest V's instruments, switches and levers. Central are the six blind-flying instruments; the engine instruments and controls are right; the undercarriage lever and throttle are left.

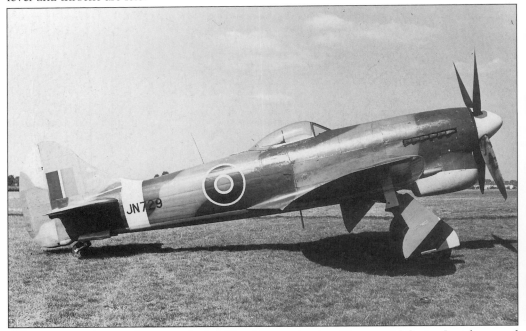

All set to put the wind up somebody! The first production Tempest V Series I with curved dorsal fin at Langley in June 1943.

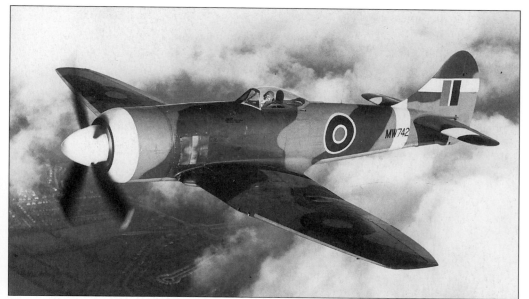

The 1943 Tempest II broke the mould with a 2520 hp Bristol Centaurus radial engine. HAL and Bristol Aeroplane Co. built 454. They served mainly with RAF squadrons overseas.

An historic meeting in April 1944. Rolls-Royce top brass visited Kingston to 'sell' to their opposite numbers at Hawker their conviction that the jet engine was the power unit of the future. Left to right: R. Lickley (HAL chief project engineer), Neville Spriggs (HAL director), E.W. Hives (later Baron Hives, R-R director and general manager), R.H. Chaplin (HAL assistant chief designer), S.G. Hooker (R-R chief engineer), W. Lappin, J.J. Ellor and R.N. Dorey (all R-R), George Bulman (HAL). Sydney Camm does not appear in this group because he took the photograph! The meeting ended a long period of 'self-inflicted antagonism' between the two companies.

Tempest V Series 2 production in full swing at Langley in July 1944 (well, it will be when all the chaps are back from lunch).

In 1947-48 India bought eighty-nine Tempest IIs and Pakistan twenty-four. All were refurbished ex-RAF aircraft. This Pakistan Tempest has underwing tanks for the ferry flight home.

The first Fury prototype to fly, in September 1944, was this one, NX798, seen here showing its partly uncowled souped-up 2,500 hp Bristol Centaurus air-cooled radial engine and four-bladed Rotol propeller.

Hawker Hot Rod. HAL's fastest piston-engined type, this Sabre-engined Fury had a 480 m.p.h. top speed. HAL built six prototypes trying to find a new joint RAF/Fleet Air Arm fighter.

This fearsome beast is another Fury prototype, the second to fly, with a Rotol six-blade contra-rotating propeller. A 2,340 hp Rolls-Royce Griffon 85 turned it.

The first Sea Fury prototype had a big 2,600 hp Centaurus engine at one end and a tiny arrester hook at the other. It first flew in February 1945.

A trials Sea Fury with wings folded is prepared for flight on HMS *Victorious* by its Fleet Air Arm crew. A Hawker engineer is seen in nearly white overalls!

Three more aspects of Sea Fury trials in HMS *Victorious* in 1946-47. With every one of the Centaurus's 2,600 horses at full gallop TF898 takes-off...

... then touches down on one wheel of its Dowty undercarriage as the arrester hook reaches down for one of the cables across the flight deck...

... and pulls the aircraft to a halt. Note that the flaps are down, the elevators are up and the canopy opened ready for a quick emergency exit.

It's all to do with camera shutter speed, aperture and engine revs! This unique photograph shows the Sea Fury's propeller blades apparently bending in different directions. They aren't.

Members of the Hawker Siddeley Aviation Board pictured during 1949. Seated, left to right: Hugh Burroughes, Sir Roy Dobson, Sir Frank Spriggs, Sir Thomas Sopwith. Standing: H. Geoffrey Herrington, J.F. Robertson, Percy G. Crabbe, -?-, -?-, Harold T. Chapman.

A Sea Fury X of the Royal Navy Historic Flight with Korean War stripes and HMS *Theseus* fin code letter. Sadly, it was lost in the sea in an accident in 1989.

Burma took delivery of eighteen Sea Fury 11 fighters and three T.20s. The periscope sight gave the instructor in the rear cockpit a good forward view.

All work and no play. Irene Bourne (later Sneddon), secretary to the pilots at the Hawker Aircraft (Blackpool) factory, with Flying Officer Joe 'Tha Hlaing of the Burmese Air Force, who helped ferry Sea Furies to Burma during 1958.

The Royal Navy Historic Flight's Sea Fury TF.20 trainer, lost in a 1990 landing accident. The elliptical wing and grouped exhausts were common to all Sea Furies.

Sea Fury TT.20 target-tower, one of eight built for Deutsche Luftfahrt Beratungsdienst during 1959-60.

K850, one of five two-seat trainer Furies sold to Pakistan in 1951-52.

Five into four will go. Ferry aircrew ready to deliver three Fury fighters, 231-233, and a two-seat trainer, 261, at the far end of the line, to Iraq.

Four
The Jet Set

The early history of the P.1040, HAL's first jet aeroplane, was similar to that of the Sea Fury. Both were designed for the RAF but ultimately were built as naval aircraft. The Sea Hawk was a single-seat single-engined interceptor and fighter/bomber, but when orders for it began to arrive, work on another new jet fighter, the Hunter, was already taking up space at Kingston. So HAL built only the first thirty-five Sea Hawks; the following 484 were produced by Armstrong Whitworth. From 1953 to 1960 Sea Hawks served with twenty FAA squadrons, five of which flew them with great skill and effect from carriers during the November 1956 Suez campaign.

A clutch of research prototypes identified only by soulless ciphers were then developed to move HAL along the jet age learning curve: first came the P.1052, virtually a swept-wing Sea Hawk; then the P.1072, a little hot rod which was the first P.1040 with a rocket motor inserted up its tail; and, finally, the P.1081 with swept wings and tail but a 'straight-through' jet pipe rather than the bifurcated type used earlier. They spanned the 1947-51 era, during which HAL acquired Dunsfold airfield in Surrey and moved all test flying there when growing civil air traffic from nearby London Airport made flying from Langley too hazardous.

The P.1067 single-seat jet fighter, first flown by Sqdn Ldr Neville Duke from Boscombe Down on 20 July 1951, became the magnificent Hunter. It epitomised Camm's continuing ability to create military aircraft with aesthetic appeal and he was knighted in 1953.

Production of Hunters began in several Hawker Siddeley Aviation factories and, as an indication of the Hunter's future performance, it set a world speed record of 727.6 m.p.h. in September 1953 flown by Neville Duke, then HAL's chief test pilot. Gun-firing at high altitude had the nasty habit of nearly choking the Rolls-Royce Avon engine to death – but this problem was cured.

With a growing order book, a factory at Blackpool's Squires Gate airfield was opened. Hunters entered RAF service with No. 45 Sqdn in July 1954 and were flown by thirty-five squadrons until withdrawal in 1962, but FAA units continued to fly them until well into the early 1980s in a variety of roles, and Hunters were exported to sixteen overseas countries.

It is said that the best marriages are made in heaven. If this be so, then heaven must be nearer than is generally thought (about halfway between Bristol and Kingston-on-Thames) because of the very special marriage of Bristol Siddeley Engines's (BSE) BE53 vectored-thrust engine with HAL's P.1127 vertical/short take-off and landing (V/STOL) aeroplane. Credit must go to BSE's technical director, Dr Stanley Hooker, who led the team which created the revolutionary engine in which the jet pipes swivelled to produce vertical and horizontal thrust, and to Ralph Hooper, a young HAL designer, who developed the airframe's design to accept this engine.

Conceived in 1958, an era of tightly tied Treasury purse strings, rationalisation and cancelled contracts, Defence chiefs were precluded from showing interest in HAL's unique aeroplane. Why? The Government had recently decided that future manned combat aircraft were 'out' and guided missiles were 'in'! Bravely, HAL decided to finance a brace of P.1127s, and when the US Mutual Weapon Development Programme agreed to cough up seventy-five per cent of the engine costs it was 'all systems go' for the aeroplane which was the basis for the Harrier.

But before the P.1127 became the Harrier there were nearly four years development flying, which enabled nine prototypes of the Hawker Siddeley Kestrel to be built to equip a tri-national evaluation squadron manned by RAF, USAF, US Army, US Navy and Luftwaffe pilots. Later, when six aircraft went to the USA, US Marine Corps pilots also flew them.

A hitherto unpublished photograph of the unmarked first P.1040 prototype, VP401, being taxied by Bill Humble at Langley. The cockpit canopy has not yet been fitted for its first flight.

Meanwhile, design work (described to the author as 'like negotiating a three-storied mine field') on the exciting P.1154, a supersonic V/STOL project went ahead, only to be cancelled by the Government. Production and development of the Harrier continued, however, the RAF's first aircraft being delivered to No. 1 Sqdn at Wittering on 1 April 1969. Deliveries of Harriers to the US Marine Corps, designated AV-8As, began in 1971. In 1976, against a tangled background of political/commercial dealing, six, designated AV-8A, went to the USA for onward transmission to Spain's Naval Air Arm, who immediately renamed them Matadors. Where there's a will...! Harrier 2 two-seat trainers were built for the RAF, US and Spain. In 1977, following Government-inspired nationalisation of Britain's aircraft industry, the name Hawker finally disappeared from the company's title, being supplanted by British Aerospace.

In September 1979 the first British Aerospace Sea Harriers were delivered to the FAA's 700A Sqdn which was commissioned at Yeovilton. It was during Operation Corporate, the 1982 Falklands War, that the importance of the Harrier/Sea Harrier was widely recognised. Operating initially from the Task Force's aircraft carriers, they played a vital role in the ultimate British victory. Sea Harriers were delivered to the Indian Navy in 1983.

US interest in Harrier development led to an agreement between HAL and McDonnell-Douglas which provided for work and information sharing on V/STOL aircraft. From this agreement came the AV-8B Harrier II, able to heft twice the load of earlier AV-8As. HAL undertook forty per cent of airframe production and Rolls-Royce sixty per cent of the engine. By combining the US and British companies' advanced know-how, much enhanced Harriers were created for the RAF. The first of these, the Harrier 5, joined No. 1 Sqdn in early 1989 and was followed two years later by the further-enhanced Harrier 7 which was equipped for night operations. These aircraft are scheduled to continue in service at least until the year 2015.

Starting life as the Hawker Siddeley P.1182, the Hawk two-seat advanced jet trainer was also a ground support aircraft, all weapons being carried externally. Duncan Simpson, chief test pilot, flew the first one on 21 August 1974 at Dunsfold. Hawk 1s joined No. 4 Flying Training School at RAF Valley in November 1976. The Hawk was the first British aircraft to be designed using metric measurements alone. In November 1979 it replaced ageing Gnat trainers used by the Red Arrows, the RAF formation aerobatic team.

Hawks have been exported to some twelve countries; they have been built and exported as both a single-seat combat aircraft and as a heavily armed combat-capable trainer. In 1984 the go-ahead was given to a new complete training system, the T45TS for the US Navy, which included a special variant of the Hawk renamed Goshawk. This contract was won in collaboration with McDonnell-Douglas which undertakes main assembly work, with British Aerospace as prime sub-contractor for the airframe and Rolls-Royce for the Adour engine.

Since work finally ceased at the Kingston site, production of the Harrier family and Goshawk wings has been carried on under the all-enveloping umbrella of British Aerospace variously at Warton, Dunsfold and Brough. The wrecking gangs moved into Richmond Road in 1993-94 and demolished the magnificent office block and factory. Strong men, all ex-employees, were, literally, in tears.

P.1040 VP401 was first flown at Boscombe Down on 2 September 1947 by test pilot Sqdn Ldr Trevor 'Wimpy' Wade, seen in the cockpit. It was to become the Sea Hawk naval interceptor fighter.

Hawker Hotter Rod. When VP401's development flying programme ended it had an Armstrong Siddeley Snarler rocket motor inserted up its tail. Renamed P.1072, it made several rocket-powered flights in 1950-51. Then official interest waned and trials ceased.

Light the blue touch paper! VP401's Snarler rocket motor undergoing ground testing. Note the diamond-shaped shock waves in the exhaust flame.

First batch of Sea Hawk F.1s being built at Armstrong Whitworth's Baginton factory in 1954. The tenth aircraft, WF182, heads the line, while Meteor production continues in the background.

A quartet of RNAS Brawdy-based Seahawk 1s of 806 'Ace of Diamonds' Sqdn pictured over the coast of West Wales in 1953.

Flt Lt Black (later Air Vice Marshal C.G. Black CB, OBE, AFC) on an exchange posting to 806 Sqdn Fleet Air Arm flying Sea Hawks, joins his carrier, HMS *Albion*, in the English Channel in September 1956.

The first Sea Hawk 2, WF240, photographed in 1954, carries ten 25 lb rocket projectiles plus a brace of 90 gallon underwing drop tanks.

In 1956 this Sea Hawk FGA.6 test flew a large mock-up underwing radar pod intended for use on German Navy Sea Hawk Mk 101 all-weather fighters.

'Up we go.' The seven-ship Sea Hawk FB.3 aerobatic team of 800 Squadron climb into a practice formation loop in readiness for their appearance in the September 1958 SBAC Display at Farnborough.

Lt John Carver's 801 Sqdn Sea Hawk gropes for HMS *Centaur*'s first cable and heads for the barrier in a wheels-up landing after undercarriage failure on 17 December 1959.

'Pilot says the battery's flat and he wants a push start.' Deck handling crew position an 898 Sqdn Sea Hawk 6 on HMS *Ark Royal*'s flight deck.

German Navy Sea Hawk Mk100s in impeccable line-abreast formation. Note the larger fin and rudder on this variant.

The Royal Navy Historic Flight's Sea Hawk 6, WV408, in July 1980. The last airworthy Sea Hawk, it has 806 'Ace of Diamonds' Sqdn markings and HMS *Albion*'s fin code letter.

HAL's first swept-wing aircraft, the P.1052, flew on 19 November 1948. This first prototype suffered several crash landings; the second became the P.1081; the last was a structural test specimen.

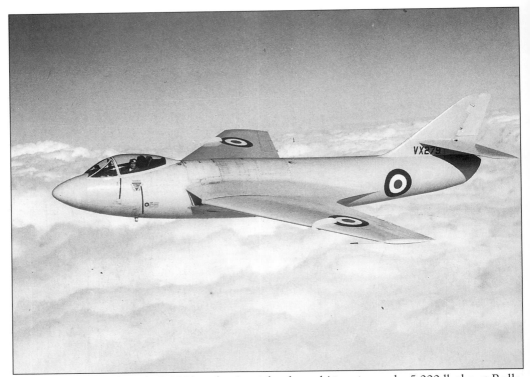

Trevor Wade flies the sole P.1081 with a 'straight-through' jet pipe and a 5,000 lb thrust Rolls-Royce Nene engine. He died when it crashed in April 1951.

Neville Duke loops the duck-egg green P.1067 Hunter in 1951. Keeping close company is Russell Adams, famed Gloster Aircraft photographer, in a two-seat Meteor 7.

Sir Sydney Camm listens intently to Neville Duke after an early test flight in the Hunter prototype in 1951.

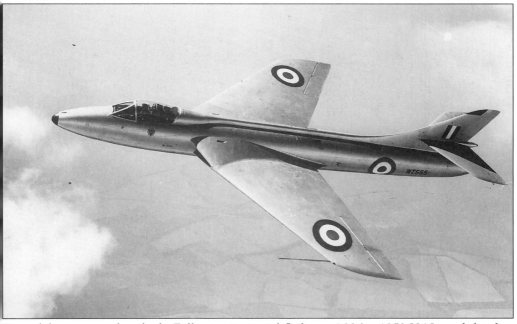

First of the umpteen hundreds. Following its initial flight on 16 May 1953 HAL used this first production Hunter F.1 for handling trials.

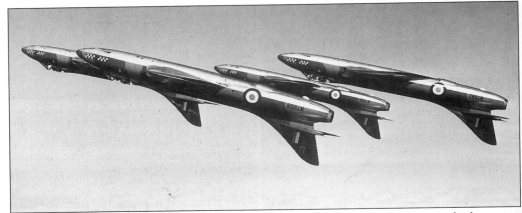

Hunter Aeros. No 54 Sqdn Hunter 1s, up from RAF Odiham, caught at the top of a formation loop. They were the official 1955 RAF aerobatic team.

A Hunter 1 shows off its newly acquired 'barn door' under-fuselage air-brake.

Scarlet Runner. The Hunter F.3 (née first prototype WB188), with pointed nose, 9,000 lb thrust Rolls-Royce Avon, painted scarlet and flown by Neville Duke, set a 727.6 m.p.h. world speed record on 7 September 1953.

Hunter production lines at the Richmond Road factory, Kingston-on-Thames in 1954.

This underside view of a Hunter 6, dramatically posed by Cyril Peckham, Hawker's chief photographer, clearly shows its 'dog-tooth' wing leading edge, empty cartridge collectors and ventral air brake.

The top view shows the Hunter's camouflage scheme. It was demonstrated in Switzerland and used for spinning trials, then had a deck-arrester hook fitted, but crashed in November 1957.

Yet another Hunter 6, with drop tanks and twenty-four rocket projectiles, none of which detract one iota from the svelte appearance of Sydney Camm's masterly design.

These members of the Hawker Siddeley Aviation Board are clearly happy with the Hunter order books. From left to right, S.D. 'Cock' Davies, Sir W.S. Farren, Sir Sydney Camm, Sir Tom Sopwith and Sir Roy Dobson are photographed in the latter's office at 18 St James Square, London.

The Hawker P.1109A, WN594, with extended nose and radome, was based on the Hunter 6. It was intended for guided missile trials

T for two. The unpainted two-pew P.1101 Hunter trainer prototype in 1955. About 100 were either built as or converted to Hunter T.7s for use by some twenty-five RAF squadrons.

Bill Bedford gave HAL's orange and white Hunter 66A demonstrator, G-APUX, a sensational public debut in the 1959 Farnborough Show. His display included twelve turns of an inverted spin!

'All work and no play....' From left to right, Bill Bedford, Grp Capt H.J. 'Willy' Wilson (sales director Blackburn Engines Co.) and George Anderson (Hawker public relations and publicity manager) relax after a hard day going about their masters' businesses.

Double Dutch. First of twenty HunterT.7s built for the Netherlands. It was first flown by HAL pilot Frank Bullen in March 1958.

Fokker licence-built ninety-three Hunter 6s during 1956-58, which equipped four squadrons of the Koninklijke Luchtmacht. Here, four of them fly an immaculate echelon right formation.

During 1958-59 HAL built twenty-two Hunter trainers like this one for the Indian Air Force.

Having bought sixteen ex-RAF Hunter 4 fighters, and after much deliberation, Peru took the plunge and ordered this sole Hunter T.62 trainer converted from another Mk 4.

Span 35 ft 0 ins. Wing Area *gross* 580 sq.

O/A Length 55 ft 0 ins.

Angle of Sweepback 65 deg. on L.E.

Fuel Capacity 800 gallons

4 x 30mm. Aden Guns 270 rounds each

P1092 HAWKER SUPERSONIC ALL-WEATHER FIGHTER
Rolls Royce Avon Engine

One of Hawker's fairly tardy 1951 contributions to the delta wing 'cult' was the P.1092 supersonic two-pew all-weather fighter project.

Not the 1956 P.1121 air superiority fighter: it's a full-scale mock-up! Prototype building began but Air Staff mind-changing pulled the rug from under this big aeroplane.

P.1127 prototype balances neatly on its Dowty 'zero-track' bicycle undercarriage. The inflatable air intake lips gave a more effective shape when hovering but deflated for horizontal flight.

The first P.1127, tethered to a gridded platform at Dunsfold in October 1960, ready for ground testing the lift generated by the Bristol Siddeley Pegasus vectored-thrust engine.

We have lift-off! On 21 October 1960 Bill Bedford made the first tethered vertical lift-off. Note the downward-pointing jet nozzles, tethering cables and aft telemetry and intercom umbilicals.

XP831, the first P.1127, in its first untethered hover on 19 November 1960. Undercarriage doors, fairings and other bits and pieces were removed to minimise weight.

As the early Pegasus engines began developing more 'muscle', the P.1127s carried more weight. Here XP831 has acquired undercarriage doors, fairings and pitot boom.

Construction of the second P.1127, XP836, in progress during 1960.

The first two P.1127s at Dunsfold in 1961. With a more powerful engine XP836 has a full complement of undercarriage doors, fairings and internal equipment.

The P.1127 twins airborne together in 1962. The second aircraft breaks away, showing its unusual planform details.

A Whirlwind 'plane guard' helicopter watches Bill Bedford, in XP831, make the world's first vertical landing by a fixed wing aircraft on a carrier at sea during February 1963.

'Goofers' fill every vantage point on HMS *Ark Royal*'s superstructure, as the P.1127 completes its historic vertical landing-on.

Commander A.R. Rawbone RN welcomes Bill Bedford aboard *Ark Royal*. Bill and HAL pilot Hugh Merewether later carried out intensive flight trials from the '*Ark*'.

Designed for NATO's needs, the P.1154 VTOL supersonic air superiority fighter was a 1964 victim of politics, the Treasury and the Royal Navy going astern on earlier enthusiasm.

A group of Sopwith Aviation and Hawker Aircraft veterans at a gathering on 21 June 1966. Standing: left to right: E.R. Comfort (Sopwith), J. Pollard (Sopwith/Hawker), J.W. Cooke (Sopwith/Hawker), R.M. Shaw (Sopwith/Hawker), ? Bowers (Sopwith), ? Bewsher (Sopwith). Seated: R.J. Ashfield (Sopwith), W. Smith (Sopwith), R. Hall (Sopwith/Hawker).

The day after the Hunter got the key of the door. On 21 July 1972, twenty-one years and one day after the Hunter first flew, a large gathering of Hawker people at Dunsfold celebrated this milestone in the history of the company and the Hunter. With an ex-RAF Hunter 6, XF422, converted to a Mk 74B, serialled 524 for the Republic of Singapore Air Force, behind them, are, left to right: A.E. O'nions, H.J. Tuffen, Neville Duke, L.L. Cross, J.V. Stanbury, H.E.J. Rochefort, F.V.K. Sutton, R.B. Marsh, L.E. Holton, B.F. Coopman, A.W. Bedford, A.E. Tagg, S.R. Bell, R.H. Chaplin, F.C. Green, D.M.S. Simpson, E.G. Rubython, J.F. White, H. Davis, D. Lockspeiser, Sir John Lidbury, R.J. Balmer, J.H. Simmonds, F.C. Lock, R. Copland, Ralph Hooper, W.A. Gold, J.S. Apted, -?-, J. Yoxall, W.S. Hollyhock, P. Jefferson, -?-, H.A.G. Waugh, J.F. Gale, W.G.H. Rayner, H.H. Hayward, W.A.C. Weetman, E.D.R. Thomas, F.W. Jeffery, H.W. Viney, J.D. Stranks, R.S. Kemp, R.E. Wigginton, R.L. Lickley, R.A. Wigginton, G. Anderson, R.E. Selwood, P.D. Betteridge, E. Rowe, T.D. Lucey, G. Jefferson.

'... and that's how we got the contract.' F.E. Sherras (left, Hawker contracts manager) in conversation with John W.R. Taylor (Editor *Jane's All the World's Aircraft*) and Albert E. Tagg (right, production engineering manager) at a talk at Kingston by former test pilot P.G. Lucas on 12 November 1973.

This dramatic photograph shows many features of the third P.1127, including the position and shape of the swivelling nozzles, the tailplane and retracted outriggers.

The sixth and last P.1127 rises vertically from a wooded clearing. It crashed and was written off when landing on 31 October 1975.

Nine developed P.1127s named Kestrel were built for an evaluation squadron with RAF, USAF and Luftwaffe pilots. Each nation was intended to acquire three Kestrels...

... but when the trials ended Germany said 'Nein'. So the USA had six. Here Kestrels are being built. Note the tripartite roundels and fin stripes.

A quintet of No. 1 Sqdn Harrier 1s in neat stepped-up echelon. The squadron received its first Harriers on 1 April 1969 while based at RAF Wittering. It is still there, in 1996, flying Harrier 5s and 7s.

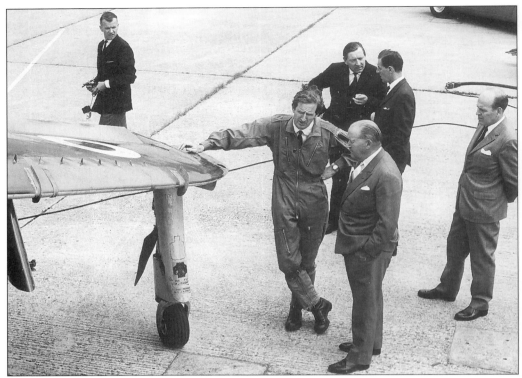

Duncan Simpson (HAL chief test pilot) and his predecessor Bill Bedford (Harrier sales manager) discuss the operational features of the Harrier with members of a Swiss Air Force delegation which visited Dunsfold in the late 1960s.

XV280, the fourth of a pre-production development batch of five Harrier 1s carries out 'dry hook-ups' during simulated flight refuelling trials with a Victor tanker aircraft. A Hunter chase plane keeps an eye on proceedings.

Harrier 1, XV758, inches forward before landing on the Commando carrier HMS *Bulwark* on 18 September 1969. The aircraft carried out brief trials with this vessel at sea.

A No. 1 Sqdn Harrier 1, with two 30 mm under-fuselage cannon pods, a pair of rocket pods and a brace of drop tanks, emerges from a leafy 'hide' in 1971. Early Harrier variants could carry a $3\frac{1}{2}$ tons war load.

A US Marine Corps AV-8A, carrying four bombs and two other disposable weapons on underwing pylons, plus a centre-line bomb and two 30 mm cannon pods.

'You take the high road...' This Harrier 1 of No. 1 Sqdn takes the low road in 1972 to show its ability to operate from unprepared sites.

This unmarked Harrier two-seater in very close company with a USMC AV-8A gives a new meaning to 'buddy-buddy' operations.

A quartet from the first batch of 12 AV-8A Harrier 50s delivered to the US Marine Corps during 1971.

Pictured in May 1973, this Harrier carries mock-ups of a new Hawker Siddeley Dynamics short range air-to-air missile launcher under its outer wings, plus a pair of drop tanks.

Wearing hastily daubed-on 'snow camouflage', this Harrier creates a mini snowstorm as it taxis out from beneath a netting 'hide' slung from surrounding trees.

Full scale mock-up of the British Aerospace/McDonnell Douglas AV-8B Harrier II photographed at MacDac's St Louis plant on 7 August 1975. Note the enlarged air-intakes, repositioned outrigger wheels and external stores.

Mock-up of the radar nose and cockpit of a Sea Harrier photographed in about 1976-77. The cockpit was eleven inches higher than the Harrier for better all-round visibility. This nose shape was test flown on a Harrier.

A Sea Harrier takes-off up the curved forward end of a Royal Navy carrier's flight deck. This technique imparted extra 'urge' to the aircraft which could then get airborne with a much heavier load than from a flat deck.

A Frazer-Nash Common Rail Launcher to suit a range of missiles was fitted to a Sea Harrier to carry this advanced medium-range air-to-air missile as a trial installation.

A Sea Harrier with the 'flying fist' marking of 899 Sqdn Fleet Air Arm in ocean-grey finish carries cannon pods, drop tanks and Sidewinder missiles. The raised cockpit and pointed nose radome are noteworthy features.

The trainer with a heavy punch. A camouflaged Hawk 1A of No. 4 Flying Training School carries a centre-line under-fuselage 30 mm cannon pod plus underwing mountings for two Sidewinder air-to-air missiles.

'Smoke on – Go.' The Red Arrows' scarlet Hawks, in their basic impeccable Diamond Nine formation, thrill and delight millions of air show spectators.

Hawks sweep across the sky turning and banking in one of their many formation sequences.

Moment of Truth. As if standing on tip-toes, its landing gear shock-absorbers fully extended, a British Aerospace/McDonnell Douglas T-45A Goshawk, the aircraft bit of the US Navy's T45 Training System, gets airborne. The Goshawk was evolved from and closely resembles the Hawk trainer.

An AV-8B hovers (note the downwards-pointing jet nozzle), revealing its undersurface lift-enhancing fore-and-aft fences with a front end air dam to contain the lift jets as they rebound from the surface during take-off.

A Harrier 5 shows off its four underwing stores carriers, raised cockpit with enlarged canopy, and restyled nose to accommodate advanced avionics and sensors. The name Flt Lt N.S.F. Gilchrist is written below the cockpit cill.

An artist's impression of what was almost the last aircraft designed at Kingston. The P.1214 project for a short take-off/vertical landing aircraft of about 1976 had the nose profile and ventral air intake of the P.1121 project of 1955. The rest was sheer Dan Dare in appearance!

Acknowledgements

Much of the pleasure in creating an historical reference work such as this stems from the personal contacts made and renewed with others with similar interests in many parts of the world. Without the help of friends who have scanned their own photograph archives, found those extra special and rare photographs, and willingly loaned them to me, you would not be holding this book in your hands today. Chief among them are Mike Hooks, who, once again, has come to my aid with gems from his seemingly bottomless collection of historical photographs, Mike Stroud, an ex-Hawker man whose knowledge of the company's business – gained at first hand – is both wide and deep, and Frank Mason who, at Sir Sydney Camm's instructions, made the first moves in gathering and collating the Hawker company's archival material.

Others who have provided important photographs are the late George Anderson who, in 1971, when he was Hawker's public relations and publicity manager, gave me free access to his photograph files; Air Vice Marshal George H. Black, who flew Sea Hawks with the Fleet Air Arm; Mrs Anne Bouillot, whose father, Alex Reid, worked at most of Hawker's factories; the late R. Fitzgibbon Carse, former 'anchor-clanker' and Gloster Aircraft Co.'s export manager; Mrs I. Sneddon, who, as Irene Bourne, worked in the pilots' office at Hawker, Blackpool; Albert E. Tagg, former production engineering manager at Kingston; and Olive Willcocks (née Cooper), who was secretary to the pilots at Brooklands 1929-36 and flew as 'live ballast' in Harts and Horseleys.

I am grateful, too, to Ivan Macquisten, editor of the *Kingston Guardian*, who enabled me to make contact again with Bill Bedford, whose contribution to aviation as Hawker's chief test pilot is immense, with Cliff Bore of Kingston Aviation Heritage, a former Hawker designer, Group Captain David Davies, a Hurricane pilot during the Battle of Britain, and with many ex-Sopwith and Hawker employees who, by letter and telephone, offered me help.

I am indebted to Alan Sutton, David Buxton and the staff of Chalford Publishing Company for their unfailing support in the creation of this book. My special thanks go once again to my wife who, having tamed our new PC and brought the software to heel, instructed my 12,000 words to adhere to a $3\frac{1}{2}$ inch diameter thin wobbly plastic disc.